..THE..

CRIME AGAINST THE YAKIMAS

By LUCULLUS V. McWHORTER

PRICE : : : : : : : : THIRTY-FIVE CENTS

...THE...

Crime Against the Yakimas

--BY--

LUCULLUS V. McWHORTER
Associate Member of the Society of American Indians

WITH

INTRODUCTION

BY

WILLIAM E. JOHNSON
Former Chief Special Officer of the United States Indian Service

FIRST EDITION

Republic Print, North Yakima, Washington

The Crime Against the Yakimas

— BY —

Lucullus V. McWhorter

Associate Member of the
Society of American Indians

To the Memory of
Ukut Ochise (Wild Eye)
The Grey Cayuse
the
Fleet Footed "Pard"
of all Our Rambles,
is this Volume Affectionately
Dedicated by the
Author.

INTRODUCTION

A S an island is defined as a tract of land entirely surrounded by
water, so may an Indian Reservation be described as a tract of
land entirely surrounded by thieves.

Too often the Indian superintendent, or agent, becomes the agent
and co-partner of those who would plunder the Indians rather than
attend to his duties as administrator of the affairs of the Indians
themselves.

The blundering, wabbling, ofttimes treacherous, administration of
Indian affairs, conducted from a seat of power three thousand miles
away, is the most sickening, discouraging, disgusting failure in the
history of American government.

While the superb, natural sense of honor of the Indian has led him
to scrupulously observe every treaty and obligation ever entered
into, the Government has left a trail of broken treaties, broken promises, repudiated pledges—an hundred years record that would dis-
grace a king of the Cannibal Islands.

What ever of relief has been obtained for the Indian has usually
been through an appeal from department red tape to the ears and
hearts of the people. Here and there is a real friend of the Abo-
rigine, who breaks bread in the wick-i-up; who feels the throbbings
of his heart; who understands him; who loves him for his virtues.
Such a man is Lucullus V. McWhorter, the writer of the pages to
follow.

Years ago McWhorter began mingling with the Yakima Indians.
He earned their confidence. He fought their battles. He aired their
wrongs in public. He spent his time and money in efforts to secure
for them a square deal. He was formally adopted into their tribe
by Chief Yoom-tee-bee, and is known among them as He-mene Ka-
wan (Old Wolf). And, while he is an adopted member of their tribe
and has participated in tribal affairs as a member of their council, he
has never sought or received one dollar of benefit from such membership.

Four years ago, when I began operations in Washington, suppress-
ing the liquor traffic among Indians, as chief officer of the Indian
service, I first crossed this man McWhorter's trail. I found him stirring them up to protest against the issuing of saloon licenses at Top-

penish. I found the Indians, under his influence, protesting against the issuing of saloon licenses at Wapato, at Parker and other places. I found him stirring up the Yakimas to petition the Secretary of the Interior, asking for the removal of the white man's saloon from their midst.

In March, 1911, a bill was introduced into the Washington senate to destroy the splendid state law against selling liquor to Indians. The news came to me immediately over the wire and I telegraphed to many persons of influence in that state, asking assistance in defeating the infamous proposal. It was L. V. McWhorter who played the card that defeated the liquor grafters. He rode the Yakima Reservation for two days. The result was, that, representing five hundred Indians, he sent a telegram to the sponsor of the bill protesting and imploring that it be withdrawn. And it was withdrawn, as the hundreds of scoundrels who have since been convicted under this law can testify.

Because of my interest in my own race as well as because of my interest in the Indian, I rejoice that the following pages have been written, and written by one so well qualified to tell the sordid story as Mr. McWhorter. If the remainder of the white race were like him, there would be no "Indian problems."

WILLIAM E. JOHNSON.

Westerville, Ohio, January 13, 1913.

The Crime Against the Yakimas

By Lucullus V. McWhorter

"INDIAN affairs are dominated by two elements—rotten politics and morbid sentimentality,'' was the recent comment by a local critic. The truth of the first accusation is patent, but had the gentleman acquainted himself more fully with the unselfish motive which prompts the comparatively few who are striving to alleviate the bitterness of the cup which has for centuries been pressed to the lips of our childlike aborigines, he certainly would not impugn all to be actuated by "morbid sentiment." However, the leaven of this force, whether morbid or otherwise, like all social and civic reforms, is being felt. There is surely "a going in the mulberry trees" for that political-ridden body holding guardianship over more than 300,000 national wards. Not in the history of the Indian Department has there been such an unearthing of mal-administration and sickening corruption. The Indian Rights Association and other eastern societies are active in protest against the criminal neglect and carnival of graft which honeycombs this branch of the Government service.

The White Earth tragedy, where the looting of the Chippewa-Ojebwa amounted to millions of dollars; the thievish usurpation by white settlers of the water rights of the Pimas; and the wholesale plundering of the Pueblos under the administration of a booze-peddling superintendent (See Note 1) shielded and abetted by the higher-ups, have at last caused all justice-loving people to cry aloud against the flagrant wrongs so wantonly inflicted upon the scattered remnant of the most mysterious and interesting race in existence. Nor do these colossal robberies stand alone. Like crimes on a minor scale are being perpetrated on almost, if not every, Indian Reservation in the United States. "Where the carcass is, there will the eagles be gathered," has been too grimly palpable in all our dealings with weaker peoples.

The Yakima Indian Reservation, Washington, was created at the Walla Walla Treaty in 1855, for the Fourteen Confederated Tribes, and covers approximately 1,000,000 acres of diversified country, including a vast body of fine desert lands susceptible to irrigation, which last has been allotted in severalty to the Indians, numbering 3,046 souls. About 42,000 acres of this is under a good system of ir-

---

NOTE 1.—See "The Story of Juan Cruz," by Wm. E. (Pussy Foot) Johnson, Former Chief Special Officer, U. S. Indian Service, Laurel, Md.

rigation, some private ditches, the canals being paid for by the Indians and by special appropriations by the government. Crops are produced on 10,000 acres additional by sub-irrigation, while perhaps 20,000 acres of the allotted lands have been purchased by the whites. This irrigable region, fertile beyond conception when watered, has long been coveted by the white man. The first attempt at irrigation on this reservation was in 1859, but our story is of later years.

In 1895 the Commercial Club of North Yakima, Wash., petitioned Congress to sell the surplus lands of the Yakimas, and to open the reservation for settlement. Two years later Commissioners were sent to negotiate with the tribe. It was estimated that 200,000 acres of land would suffice for all allotments, and for the residue the Government offered "unusually liberal terms"—$1,400,000, deferred payments to bear four per cent. interest. The Yakimas spurned this munificent (?) offer.

It is well at this point to state that for years the Indian Office sold deceased Indian lands for the advantage of the speculator rather than the actual home-seeker. The undivided allotments were offered to the highest sealed cash bidder, consequently only those well equipped could compete; result, vast and valuable holdings by a few at extremely low valuations.

In 1909 I brought these conditions to the notice of the Indian Department and was promised that a change would be made; that the allotments would be subdivided and sold on terms. Not until February, 1911, was there any change; since which time, at the Indians' request, terms are granted, but no subdivisions. It is well recognized that lands in this valley sell at higher values in small tracts. The fallacy of the all-cash sales is apparent when it is understood that in nearly every case the money is doled out to the beneficiary in meager monthly installments. Thousands of dollars have been lost to the Indians by this criminal stupidity of the Department.

Aside from the Jones bill, December 21, 1904, referred to elsewhere in this volume, which provides for the opening of the Reservation and the sale and settlement of unallotted tribal lands, the next serious attempt to amputate the Yakimas from their lands, culminated in the

Notorious Jones Bill

March 6, 1906, which provides that the irrigable lands of the Reservation be cared for by the United States Reclamation Service. This bill, with the consent of the Indian, authorizes the Secretary of the Interior to sell sixty acres of each eighty-acre allotment; the twenty acres retained by the Indian to be furnished with a water right, to be paid for from the sale of the sixty acres. After the payment of such water right, "the balance, if any, shall be deposited in the treasury of the United States, to the credit of the individual Indian, and may be paid to any of them, if, in the opinion of the Secretary of the Interior such payments will tend to improve the condition and advance the progress of said Indian, but not otherwise." Under this act the Wapato Project to water about 120,000 acres, was launched.

The estimated cost for a water right for the Indian's twenty acres, including storage, is $30.00 per acre.

It would be jocund, if it were not so tragical, to read the report of the Indian Committee, urging the passage of the Jones bill:

"In this way," says the report, "the lands will be reclaimed and settled and the Indian will have a good and perpetual water right for his remaining 20 acres of land, which is more than he is apt to cultivate and is worth more than 80 acres of unirrigated land. With an absolute assurance that a good water right can be secured the value of the 60 acres which he can sell will be greatly increased.

"Purely agricultural lands similar in character to these and in the same neighborhood are now worth from $150 to $800 per acre. * * * They produce alfalfa from three to four crops a year; hops, a ton and a quarter per acre; potatoes and vegetables of all kinds; the finest of apples, peaches, pears, plums, apricots, prunes, and fruits of all kinds other than tropical or semitropical. With water these lands will be just as valuable and produce the same kind of crops. They lie adjacent to

SUB-IRRIGATED MEADOW.
Yakima Indian Reservation.
Well and Sweat House.
(Copyrighted by the Author.)

the Northern Pacific Railway line. Climatic conditions are splendid. The winters are mild, and the summers have warm days, pleasant nights, and almost continual sunshine. The markets of Puget Sound are but eight hours distant.

"In this section the lands under irrigation are cut up into small farms of from 5 to 40 acres each. Many families own but 10 acres, from which they make a good living and save money. If each Indian were to take advantage of this bill he would still retain 20 acres—that is, a family of four would have a farm of 80 acres. It is a good thing to allow the Indians to dispose of a portion of their allotments and thereby surround themselves with energetic, industrious farmers. They will be able to secure all the work they desire. They will have the example and reward of industry ever before them, and if anything will promote their civilization this will do it. The bill is for the benefit of the Indians, and will not cost the Government a dollar. Its passage will also assist materially in the development of irrigation in the Yakima Valley."

Eliminating the Indian Factor.

"After a careful consideration of the bill," wrote Indian Commissioner F. E. Leupp, in recommending its passage to the Secretary of the Interior, "I am convinced that if it is enacted the 'Indian factor' in the Yakima Valley project will be eliminate (See Note 2) and the Reclamation Service can carry that project out."

Louis Mann, a full blood Yakima, who will be referred to often in this article, saw in the local press the trend of the Jones bill and wrote a protest to Senator Ankeny, signed jointly by himself and his clan chieftain, and received the following communication:

NOTE 2.—Commissioner Leupp was resourceful in methods of "eliminating the Indian factor." In 1907, upon his recommendation, By-a-lil-li and seven other Navajos were transported from the Navajo Reservation to Huachuca, Arizona, where, "without any charge having been filed against them in any court of law, and without the benefit of council or procedure by due course of law, they were confined in a military prison for an indefinite period at hard labor." Eighteen months later, upon habeas corpus proceedings instituted by the Indian Rights Association, they were ordered released by the Superior Court of Arizona. (See Senate Document No. 118, 60th Congress, 1st Session.)

"House of Representatives,

"Mr. Lewis Mann,   Washington, D. C., March 21, 1906.
"Mr. Weyahnp Wayaeika, Indians,
                    "North Yakima, Washington.
"Gentlemen:

"Your letter of March 6 to Senator Ankeny, protesting against my bill, has been shown to me by the Senator and I cannot believe that you understand this bill. I have been pressing the matter more out of friendship for the Indians, and for the good it would be to them, than otherwise and I wish you, or some one for you, would point out in what respect it is an injury to you. It does not compel you to sell any of your land, for you can hold your land just the same as you are now holding it and just as long as you live if you want to or, if you would prefer it, you can sell sixty acres of your allotment. I have never heard a word of protest from any one with reference to this bill and I assure you that if you had any objection to it and had presented it to me it would have been considered. I think that, if you will look the bill over or have it explained to you by some one who will give you the real meaning of it, you will see that your interests have been looked after.   "Respectfully yours,
                                    "W. L. JONES."

This explanation (?) failed to convince the recipients that Mr. Jones had "been pressing the matter more out of friendship for the Indians than otherwise." No previous protest had been made for the very good reason that the tribe knew nothing of this philanthropic move, nor had they a white friend sufficiently interested in their welfare to apprise them of the impending danger To this day the primary influence which prompted Mr. Jones to exert himself so munificently in their behalf is an unsolved mystery to the Yakimas. Chief Saluskin, We-owikt, a primitive pagan, said: "I hear that Jones made speech in Congress and told: 'We will make Christians of the Yakimas; they must do heap praying and twenty acres is all they will have time to work.' "

The true incentive to the Jones bill is found in

CHIEF SA-LUSKIN WE-OWIKT, 1911.
"My Father was once chief of all this country and my tribe was strong."
(Copyrighted by the Author.)

a study of the correspondence of that period on file in the Indian Office. The Reclamation Service wanted a foothold in the Yakima Reservation, but the unsettled condition of the water rights of the Indians was a stumbling block.

Beginning at Union Gap, the Yakima river bounds the Reservation on the east a distance of about forty miles. Notwithstanding that the treaty of 1855 "secures" to the confederated tribes and bands of Indians "the exclusive right of taking fish in all the streams running through or bordering said Reservation," this recognition of the priority right of the Yakimas to this stream avails them nothing. The Reclamation Service refers to the Indians' contention for irrigation water as "vague claims."

In 1891 the Northern Pacific, Kittitas and Yakima Irrigation Company began constructing a dam across the Yakima river some three miles below Union Gap for the purpose of diverting water to a canal irrigating a large tract of land northeast of this stream. Under date of October 8, 1891, Major Jay Lynch, then Indian Agent for the Yakima Reservation, wired the Indian Commissioner notice of this infringement of the rights of the Yakimas, not only appropriating water which was rightfully theirs, but also seriously interfering with their fishing rights. On Nov. 17, 1891, the Acting Commissioner advised the Secretary of the Interior of the probable effect of this diversion dam, and recommended that the District Attorney for the State of Washington make a full investigation and institute suits if necessary, for infringement on the Indian Rights, stop the construction of the dam and have it removed. However, no steps were taken to stay the erection

MAJOR JAY LYNCH
Photo during incumbency as Yakima
Indian Agent.

of this dam, which was in gross violation of the Government's treaty obligation to protect its dependent wards. In consequence, practically the entire flow of the Yakima river during the vital irrigating season is diverted to this alien canal and the Indians are compelled to buy storage water from the Reclamation Service, or lose heavily on their crops. This piracy has greatly retarded the development of their lands, leaving thousands of acres in sagebrush that are accessible to the canals already constructed.

"Killing" the Waneto Slough.

A short distance below this dam was a stream of some magnitude, known as the Waneto Slough, running from the Yakima river across the Reservation valley to Toppenish creek on the south. Several Indians and a few white renters had built laterals along this stream, conducting water to a considerable body of land. Except at the time of the spring floods, this branch of the Yakima river has been dry since the construction of the dam, entailing loss and misery to the allottees with no hope of redress. A few years prior, when the Northern Pacific Railroad was built across the Reservation, this stream, or creek, was bridged, permitting the unobstructed flow of the water. Subsequently, to obviate the expense of maintaining this bridge, the railroad company proceeded to fill the channel with earth. Mr. Lynch protested on the ground that it was a natural stream from which water had been appropriated by the Indians for irrigation purposes. The railroad company desisted and the bridge is still there.

In 1894 the Northern Pacific, Kittitas and Yakima Irrigation Company went into the hands of a receiver and was reorganized as the Washington Irrigation Company, since which time its canal has been known as the Sunnyside Canal.

In 1897 the intake of the two main Reservation canals provided for 314 cubic feet per second. Their combined length, 15.47 miles, with 13.66 miles of laterals, covered 30,000 acres. Waneto Slough provided for 200 cubic feet per second, making a total of 514 second feet. (Report of Commissioner of Indian Affairs, 1897, L. T. Erwin, Agent.)

With additional laterals from these various sources fully 50,000 acres of the very best soil can be irrigated.

On Feb. 19, 1903, in addition to the riparian rights of the Yakimas, Mr. Lynch, under the State laws, filed on 1,000 cubic feet per second flow of water at Union Gap for the use of the Reservation lands.

In 1904 a move was on foot to transfer the Sunnyside Canal to the United States under the Reclamation Service. On May 4, 1905, this bureau withdrew the unappropriated waters of the Yakima river under the State Water Appropriation Law of March 5, 1905. In August, 1905, the Reclamation engineers made an estimate of the low water flow in the Yakima river at Union Gap, showing a minimum of 793 cubic feet per second. The flow in the Sunnyside canal and the Reservation canals, including Waneto Slough, were also measured. The result is here given:

	Amount diverted Aug., 1904	Amount diverted Aug., 1905.
Sunnyside Canal	605 cu. ft. per second	624 cu. ft. per second
Reservation Canals	226 cu. ft. per second	269 cu. ft. per second

This table is from the Fourth Annual Report of the Reclamation Service, 1904-5.

Below are given figures by the same bureau in its Fifth Annual Report, 1906:

	Average diversion Aug., 1905.	Flow latter part of Aug., 1905.
Sunnyside Canal	626 cu. ft. per second	650 cu. ft. per second
Reservation Canals	269 cu. ft. per second	147 cu. ft. per second

In this second report, covering the same period, a new column of figures appears wherein the Sunnyside canal gained 24 second feet of water while the Reservation canals lost 122 second feet. By what process of legerdemain this result was evolved, we leave for the Reclamation Service experts in mathematical jugglery to explain.

It is noted that the flow in the Reservation canals is reported as a unit; but were they.

Compared with Agent Erwin's report in 1897, they were not; and the figures of the Reclamation Service are false. In any event, as previously shown, the Waneto Slough was dry from the diversion by the Sunnyside canal at the time of this measurement; nor are some private ditches included. In the report for 1904, for the evident purpose of detracting attention from the purloining of its waters, this stream is called

"Gilbert's Canal."

Mr. H. M. Gilbert, a prominent commission merchant and Reservation real estate broker, had leased and irrigated lands from this slough, and, as will hereafter be seen, was conspicuous in fighting for the Reclamation Service in the Reservation. Mr. Lynch, under date of February 3, 1906, called the attention of the Indian Office to this grossly fallacious modern name, showing that the stream is a natural one; and that the Indians were suffering because of the misappropriation of its water by the Washington Irrigation Company. He warned the office that unless the natural flow was restored, litigation was likely to follow. No attempt has ever been made to have the stolen water returned to this per white man "Gilbert's Canal."

In 1905, in accordance with an agreement or silent acquiescence of the Indian Department, the Secretary of the Interior adjudicated the water rights of the Indians and the Washington Irrigation Company on the basic figures of the "magic column" appearing in the Report of the Reclamation Service, 1906, previously cited. He "tacitly" gave to the irrigation company 650 cubic feet, which is sufficient to irrigate approximately 60,000 acres, and generously conceded the 147 cubic feet to the Indians, which will irrigate not to exceed 12,000 acres. This ruling seems all the more criminal when we realize that the Sunnyside canal at that time covered only 60,000 acres, since increased to 100,000 acres, which is all the land available; while the Wapato Project embraces 120,000 acres.

On the Ahtanum, a boundary stream tributary to the Yakima, the Indians were permitted to retain only a fourth of the low water flow, leaving the old Indian ditches constructed some thirty years previously, entirely dry. Complaint to the department avails them nothing.

Justice had no component part in this "dividing of the waters" of the Yakima. It was in reality an official confirmation of the theft of the Reservation waters, amounting to undetermined millions of dollars. This "adjustment" was regarded as final and a strong score for the Reclamation Service in foisting upon the Government in a very questionable deal — the taking over of the Sunnyside canal. The Interior Department could not, however, consider this purchase until a "clear slate" for the Reclamation Service on the Yakima Reservation was apparent, and to this end the Jones bill, March 6, 1906, was formulated and passed. On the 27th day of the same month the Secretary of the Interior closed the contract which had been drawn the previous year, for the Sunnyside canal in the sum of $250,000 cash and a retained water right for 9,000 acres then supposed to be under irrigation, which, however, materialized only 7,000 acres.

Mr. Lynch bitterly opposed this move. Under date of February 3, 1906, he sent a lengthy protest to Mr. W. H. Code, (See Note No. 3) Inspector of Indian Service, and to the Commissioner of Indian Affairs. He said in part:

"The Yakima River is a boundary stream and the treaty gives certain exclusive rights to this stream to the Indians, and must necessarily give the United States exclusive jurisdiction and control of the waters of this stream. The Washington Irrigation Co., the largest user of water on the river, has constructed a dam across the Yakima River upon Indian lands, and have appropriated a large amount of water under the state law, without any act of Congress granting them this right or privilege, when in fact the state had disclaimed any jurisdiction over it. (See Note 4) and it was and is impossible for this company to secure any right or title without an act of Congress, and they now propose to sell to the U. S. their plant and water rights. I think it would be well for the Government to investigate their title to water and dam before they purchase from this company."   *   *   *

"As stated in my former letter, I do not think the Jones Bill as now pending makes a clear slate, nor attempts to say what water rights the Indians have, or how much storage they will require, which is all a matter of guess, and if not determined now, it will have to be settled some time, probably by the courts."

Upon the consummation of the sale of the Sunnyside canal, the Reclamation Service entered the reservation and proceeded to survey and map out the "Wapato Project," including storage dams in the mountains. This work was completed in two years at a cost of about $36,000, and early in 1908 Mr. Lynch was importuned by the Indian Department and local promoters as to the probable outcome of securing the Indians' signatures to contracts for water rights. He was urged to do all in his power to insure success. Mr. H. M. Gilbert, the henchman of the Reclamation Service, wrote him that he understood that the matter of watering the Reservation was up to his getting the consent of the Indians. "I had understood," he continues, "that the

NOTE 3.— Mr. Code, then Acting Chief Engineer of the Indian Service, disclaims any part in the "adjudication" of the Reservation boundary waters. The division was made arbitrarily and without his consent. As a substance of fact, Mr. Code was, at the time, Consulting Engineer for the Reclamation Service.

NOTE 4.—Art. XXVI of the Constitution of the State of Washington, reads:

"That the people inhabiting this state do agree and declare that they forever disclaim all right and title to the unappropriated public lands lying within the boundaries of this state, and to all lands lying within said limits owned or held by any Indian or Indian tribes; and that until the title thereto shall have been extinguished by the United States, the same shall be and remain subject to the disposition of the United States."

Secretary of the Interior was authorized to sign contracts for this water for the Indians as wards of the government." He criticised Mr. Lynch for the delay. Mr. Lynch had vainly tried to ascertain the probable cost of the Wapato Project, but true to the "gum shoe" policy of the Reclamation Service, this information was withheld.

In a letter dated June 8, 1908, to the Indian Commissioner, Mr. Lynch says:

"I believe that your Office as well as this office has always contended and believed that the Reservation is justly entitled to a good portion of the natural flow of the Yakima River, it being a boundary stream of the Reservation, and if we have such a right now is the time to contend for it and it seems unjust to the Indians that the proceeds of the sale of their land should be expended in the construction of reservoirs to furnish water. It is my opinion that if they are entitled to even one-half of the flow of the Yakima River, they would not need any storage water or have any use for reservoirs and dams."

Again, under date of June 11, 1908, he wrote the Commissioner:

"It may be useless to contend for any more of the flow of the Yakima River than the Reclamation Service feel disposed to allow the Reservation, but the division which they seem to think is settled upon certainly seems to me to be unfair and unjust and I am at a loss to understand upon what basis any such division could be based, and if we have to accept it, it means that the reservation lands must bear nearly all of the cost of the construction of dams for storage which will probably be somewhere between $1,000,000 and $2,000,000, just how much no one at this time seems to know.

"I doubt very much whether the natural flow of the Yakima River can be legally taken from the reservation and these Indians deprived of their treaty rights without an act of Congress and perhaps even an act of Congress could not deprive the owners of land of rights they were legally possessed of. However, it is not my intention to argue this matter, but the Reclamation Service will find that they are going to have a great deal of trouble in securing contracts for the Wapato Project on the basis of the division as stated in the enclosed letter."

The Jones Bill a "Gold Brick."

Under date of June 20, 1908, he continues:

"I have always understood from Mr. Code that the matter of the division of the water of the Yakima River was not entirely settled upon and that he had never recommended or agreed to a division as claimed by the Reclamation Service, and to tell the truth I have always felt that the delegation in Congress from this state and the Reclamation Service in recommending the buying of the Sunnyside Canal recommended that the government purchase something, especially in the way of the Sunnyside water right and dam, that they already owned or held in trust for the Indians. The Secretary had stated prior to the approval of this purchase that they must show a clear slate as to the water rights and especially as to the Yakima Indian Reservation, and the bill known as the Jones Bill, placing the reservation lands under the Reclamation Project, was largely in the nature of a gold brick passed up to the Secretary to make him think there was a clear slate, and as soon as the Sunnyside property was purchased it was generally admitted by the Reclamation Service, as well as others, that this bill could not be put into effect or operation without some amendments and the amendments that the Reclamation Service want and are trying to get is that the Secretary be authorized to dispose of 60 acres of their land in accordance with the Jones bill without the consent of the Indians, at least their attorney so informed me that they were trying to get such an act passed by Congress. There was a law passed (See Note 5) opening the Reservation and the Indians were not consulted nor their

NOTE 5.—Act of December 21, 1904. Bill introduced by Congressman W. L. Jones. See Note 7, this volume. Act of December 21, 1904. Bill introduced by Congressman W. L. Jones. See Note 7, this volume.

consent given and they naturally feel pretty sore about this matter and on account of the feeling existing on this account it makes it pretty hard to talk with them about getting their consent on any question. This irrigation matter is not a question for council but the individual Indians have to be dealt with, and they as a rule are so ignorant about such matters and many of them can't even talk the English language, that it is not going to be an easy task to get their consent and if a success is made of the matter it must be done by some person who has had some experience in dealing with Indians and who can give the matter his whole time and attention."

It was evident that Mr. Lynch was not in harmony with this gigantic steal; and upon refusing to be transferred, or to resign, he was, on January 1, 1909, "suspended" from office and Mr. S. A. M. Young installed in his place. This gentleman was then in perfect accord with the coalition of the Reclamation Service and the Indian Department, and the following spring was marked by general activity along the entire line. The final coup of securing the Indians' consent to the selling of his sixty acres was at hand.

The Yakimas as a unit knew nothing of the import of the Jones bill until I explained it to them at a council called by the late Chief Yoom-tee-bee, June 9, 1909. In this council a petition to the Indian Commissioner for a redress of various grievances was formulated, from which the following is copied:

"Complaint 6. Regarding the disposal of sixty acres of the allotted eighty, the Indians think that they should be permitted to retain at least one-half of their eighty acres, and hope for an amendment to the Act in question, to that effect.

"They realize that the white man can hold forty acres under the government irrigation system, on the Tieton near North Yakima, and they feel the injustice of any legislation which compels them to relinquish, or dispose of, three-fourths of their land, under pain of being deprived of all water rights."

"Twenty Acres Enough for an Indian."

I also wrote Senator Jones:

"The Indians feel that they have not been justly treated in this matter. * * Many of them have constructed private ditches and have their lands under cultivation. They were encouraged to do this, believing that such improvements would be permanent, and that the water was theirs and would never be taken from them.

"They now hope for an amendment to the act in question, which will permit them to hold forty acres instead of twenty, and are looking to you to champion their cause. This is not an unreasonable request, and we trust that you will do all in your power to accomplish this end. It should be borne in mind that the Yakimas are not a generation from the 'hunter state' and are wholly incapable of the scientific farming so absolutely necessary for a livelihood on a twenty-acre tract.

"Under the conditions now being forced upon him, he can never hold his own with the resourceful white man whose greed and avarice seem to be insatiate."

Mr. Jones replied:

"There will be no possibility of passing any legislation of this kind amending the act permitting the sale of 60 acres at the present session of Congress, nor do I think it possible to pass it at any time. The Indian does not have to sell any of his allotment if he does not want to do so, and knowing as much about the Indian and irrigation as you do, I am satisfied you will agree with me that 20 acres of irrigated land is about all any Indian would be able to properly manage and if he can sell the 60 acres and, out of the proceeds get a water right for the remaining 20 acres and still have a little surplus remaining to help him along, it seems to me he ought to be in pretty good shape."

In March, prior to this, I had, at the instance of Chief Yoom-tee-bee, forwarded to the Indian Office a protest similar to the foregoing, to which the Commissioner replied under date May 7, 1909:

"The Office believes that twenty acres of irrigable land on the Yakima Reservation is ample for the needs of any allottee, and that the sale of the larger quantity will enable him to make better use of the twenty acres retained.

"Special Agent Charles E. Roblin, has been detailed to the Yakima Reservation to explain to the Indians the purport of the legislation, and to endeavor to obtain from them petitions for the sale of the excess lands.

"Mr. Roblin has the confidence of the Yakima Indians and is the person best fitted to deal with them in this matter."

Mr. Roblin had acted as chief clerk of the Yakima Agency, and the Indians were very well acquainted with him. To the surprise of the Indian Office, his efforts fell flat. But few Indians could be induced to sign. Mr. Roblin was later removed and has since figured in the Pima water scandals in Arizona.

In the latter part of July, 1909, the opposition of the allottees to the undertaking became so manifest that Mr. C. F. Hauke, then chief clerk of the Indian Office, visited the Reservation to ascertain the hindering cause. He soon expressed his belief that there was "some outside influence at work among the Indians."

It is true that simultaneous with Mr. Roblin's advent, that Wild Eye, the Grey Cayuse, and rider was hitting the Reservation trails hard, creating a dust which proved a veritable hoodoo to that worthy's most strenuous efforts at collecting Indian autographs.

YAKIMA INDIAN HUNTERS, 1912.
Breaking Camp on the Desert.—Wild Eye, "The Grey Cayuse,"
(Copyrighted by the Author.)

The promoters of the Wapato canal were now in despair. They saw their pet scheme of "civilizing" the half hunter, half pastoral Yakima by confining him to a twenty-acre garden among a dense population of "energetic and industrious" white farmers, go glimmering. Something should be done for the "poor Indian"; so, in July, 1909, Mr. Gilbert, the Reservation real estate broker, and two associates, under the auspices of the Commercial Club of Toppenish, a Reservation town, advocated in the press and petitioned the Secretary of the Interior:

"That it would be better to follow the advice of former Commissioner Leupp and give such Indians as do not want to take advantage of the Jones bill, patents in fee simple and treat the allotted Indians as they really are, American citizens."

This, when interpreted, reads: "Then the white man with much booze and very little money will speedily 'eliminate' the 'Indian factor' from the Yakima Valley forever."

Great scheme! (See Note 6.) I took exceptions, which at once made apparent the source of the "outside influence at work among the Yakimas." I was then approached by Mr. Gilbert with a modified form of contract, or petition, empowering the Secretary of the Interior to "dispose of such lands of above described allotment as may be necessary," for a water right in the proposed irrigation sytsem. He urged that the entire improvement could be paid for from the sale of timber and unallotted lands, which are to be sold under the Jones Act of December 21, 1904. This I then believed, and still deem feasible, and I could see no justice in the Government's exacting further security from its wards which places them at the mercy of unscrupulous landsharks.

However, notwithstanding that this petition

BILLY STAHAI (1911).
Sub-Chief and Councilman.
"Me-yay-wah (God) created the water for all."
(Copyrighted by the Author.)

when signed, authorizes the sale of sixty acres of each allotment if "necessary" and that great abuses were likely to result to the detri-

NOTE 6.—The Reservation Real Estate Broker proved an eager follower of the humane (?) Leupp, who, in 1908, advocated and urged Congress to pass an act repudiating all treaty stipulations wherein the Government holds in trust for a period of

ment of the Indian, I felt that it was a losing game for the tribe to let its lands remain idle; that the white man was gradually absorbing them at speculative prices—this coupled with the statement to me by one in the game, that "Within five years the white man will have such control as to enable him to build the canal regardless of the Indians' consent"; from another, that "The Indian may as well understand at once that the government will build this canal whether

WILLIAM CHARLEY.
Interpreter (1912)
(Copyrighted by the Author.)

the Indians want it or not." All this considered, I deemed it just as well at that time for the allottees to sign and take chances.

I accordingly called the tribe in council and had the import of the

twenty-five years, the patent of an allottee; and to authorize the Secretary of the Interior, "at his discretion," to issue to any Indian who may refuse to send his children to school, or any Indian who persists in drunkenness, a patent in fee simple for his land, and leave him "to take care of himself as best he can."—(See House Document No. 790, 60th Congress, 1st Session.)

This would place beyond the protection of the Government the most ignorant and the most helpless class of Indians, leaving them a ready prey to that law-defying combination, the bootlegger and the land grabber.

new petition fully explained. The Indians hesitated. They could not
understand this sudden interest of the white man in the welfare of
his despised red brother. Why had the petition been changed? Was
not an amendment to the Jones bill refused? There must be some
trap? Louis Mann wrote me, "If Mr.

Indians Are Squeezed to Hell

they will never give no consent to their allotments be sold as the
Jones bill is. This is no fooling among my nation of Yakima Indians.
I am in earnest; I have been talking to my people and every one con-
cerned do not wish none of that business."

It was arranged for the Indian council to meet the Hon. R. A. Ballinger, Secretary of the Interior, in North Yakima, the evening of
August 24, 1909. In the interval it was highly desirous that some
showing of actual work be presented to the Secretary upon his ar-
rival; and with this in view, Mr. Gilbert proposed to William Charley,
a full blood Indian, and the writer, that if said William Charley
would come to his office in Toppenish and act as interpreter in securing signatures to these new petitions, he would place all such petitions
in his fire safe "until the Indians are entirely satisfied to have them
sent to Washington," but if at any time the Indians were not satisfied, he would upon our request, surrender the petitions to be destroyed.

With this understanding William Charley began work, and secured
several signatures to the petitions, which were left in the gentleman's
care as agreed. The Indians were never fully satisfied with this work,
and afterwards we made a written demand for the return of the petitions in question, which demand was silently ignored. We were
trapped. The gentleman failed to keep his word of honor.

Indian Council Meets Secretary Ballinger.

The Indian Council convened at my house August 24, 1909, and
completed a petition which was in part prepared at a previous council, to Mr. Ballinger, setting forth some of their grievances and praying for relief, which never came. Owing to the death of a relative,
Chief Yoom-tee-bee did not attend this council. Two orators,
Chiefs Meninock and Shut-to-monen (Charley Wesley) were chosen to
lay before the Secretary, the Council's view of the proposed Wapato
canal, through William Charley as interpreter. Superintendent
Young, a few Indian and Reclamation Service officials, including Mr.
Gilbert, and others, were present.

Chief Meninock spoke briefly, setting forth their right to one half
of the water in the Yakima river. He referred to the treaty of 1855
to which his father was a signer; that they had tried to live up to
their part of this compact and that the whites should do likewise. He
plead earnestly that they be not further wronged by the government;
that they be permitted to retain all their lands, which they loved as an
ancestral heritage. The Indians did not want to sell any of their land.

Mr. Ballinger turned to the interpreter and said: "Tell him that they do not have to sell any of their land. I will water it and let them keep it all."

Surprised and angered at such a mendacious statement, I interposed: "Excuse me, Mr. Secretary, but if the Indians sign the petition in question, can you not sell up to sixty acres of each allotment so watered if necessary?"

"Well, yes," was the hesitating reply: "I suppose that I can if necessary, but it is not likely to be necessary."

This little episode did not tend to allay the well founded suspicions of trickery already in the minds of the Indians. They had at a previous tribal council accused Mr. Roblin of securing signatures of those who did not understand the nature of the petition, and they now felt that the entire scheme was a well laid plot in the Jones bill to absorb their lands. I am free to confess that from this time on my zeal in the success of the undertaking lagged, and subsequently I rejoined the hostiles.

Shut-to-monen was not permitted to speak. His time was usurped by a prominent local attorney who gratuitously enlightened the Secretary as to the great wealth of some of the Yakimas and how they should be given patents in fee for their lands. This gentleman afterwards publicly advised the Secretary that the present irrigation system on the reservation, which cost the Indians about $150,000, should be taken over by the Reclamation Service, the cost money refunded to the Indians, to be then used in building reservation roads. This principle of loot is in perfect harmony with subsequent movements along this line.

The Fort Simcoe Council

In September, 1909, a council was held at Fort Simcoe, where the opposition of the Indians was strongly manifested. Supt. Young was an early speaker. He told them that according to his estimate, it would only take from seven to twenty acres of each allotment watered, in addition to the tribal funds, to secure individual water rights; and that this amount was all that would be sold, if they would sign the contracts. This statement was seemingly received with bad faith, as Klah-toosh, an hereditary chief, arose and said:

"Yes, my friend; I understand your talk. Do not bring any lies that you can manufacture. This country is ours. The water is ours. The law knows this. Who gave you the right to take from us our water which is life, and then offer it back to us in exchange for our land? Why should we pay for that which always belonged to us? You white people want to eat us up like hogs. Do not talk to us like fools."

In this connection Mr. Young subsequently said to this Council, "Let it be known once for all that the Indians can keep all their lands if they want to do so."

Lumni, the aged scout, replied, comparing Mr. Young to Gov. Stevens. "When Governor Stevens made treaty with our fathers in 1855, he said, 'So long as the sun shines, so long as Mt. Adams stands

CHIEF YOOM TEE-BEE. (Bitten by a grizzly bear.)
Leader of the "Hostiles."
"You are now my brother. You must always stand by my people and help them."

and so long as the water flows down to the ocean, will this reservation be yours.' Now like Governor Stevens, you come with sugar in your mouth and talk two ways. We want no lies."

Judge Louis Simpson said that he would never sign until he was satisfied that the pledges made would be kept. He referred to the promise of the Northern Pacific Railroad in securing the right-of-way through their reservation, that they would be given "free passage and free transportation for their farm products," which promises were never made good. In no uncertain words he charged bad faith on the part of all white men wherever they had had dealings with them.

Mr. Gilbert, the reservation real estate broker, the gentleman who advocated fee-patents for the Indian lands; he who held in trust the signed up petitions, now stood up and in a long harangue explained how the lands watered could be made to pay for the full water rights from rentals alone. He made the astounding statement that "under the contracts the Indians cannot lose any part of their lands, even though none of their timber is sold; if only they will sign up." He kindly offered to meet them in council at any time and explain all points connected with the contracts not fully understood.

It was then that Chief Yoom-tee-bee arose with native dignity and in part said: "I have heard that talk before. I feel sweetened. This Government keeps not its word with us. At the Wenatchee treaty we were promised money; but our lips are dry. We have never seen that money. We want to see this money first; then we will decide about this other business. We older men are not satisfid to sign. When we gaze on that money we will say, 'Now let us consider this question.'"

He declared: "We do not want Mr. Gilbert to come to our councils and tell us what to do. We know our own business. We know what we want, and we want no blind talk."

Mr. Young explained that the Wenatchee money would be only ten dollars for each Indian; and urged the futility of permitting such trifling matter to stand in the way of so important business as irrigation for their lands. Chief Yoom-tee-bee replied, "The Wenatchee money belongs to us. It has not been paid. I am not ready to sign until this is settled. I do not ask instructions from you. I want nothing crooked for my people. There are," he added significantly, "some points not yet settled. The Cedar Valley was taken from us and never paid for. (See Note 7.) When all is clear, I will sign." Nothing was accomplished at this council.

Chief Yoom-tee-bee subsequently said: "These men, working

NOTE 7.—Owing to an erroneous western boundary line, approximately 200,000 acres of the Yakima Reservation, including the Cedar Valley, was long in dispute; and a great many settlers homesteaded the best part of the valley in question. On December 21, 1904, the Jones bill was passed, authorizing the opening of the Yakima Reservation and the sale and settlement of unallotted lands. This bill recognizes the Indian claim to the disputed territory, but it provides: "That where valid rights have been acquired prior to March 5, 1904, to lands within said tract by bona fide settlers or purchasers under the public land laws, such rights shall not be abridged, and any claim of said Indians to these lands is hereby declared to be fully compensated for by the expenditure of money heretofore made for their benefit and in the construction of irrigation works on the Yakima Indian Reservation." This bill was hard to put water on my reservation; it is for themselves and not the Indians. They are making money out of Indian lands; they care not for us. They never come to our homes to see how we are getting along; nor do they try to help us. They have built towns on my reservation and filled them with saloons. They are killing my people with whiskey. Our agent never comes among us, but reports to Washington that we have houses like the white man, and are doing well. This is not so. Some Indians get little rent money, and build house same as chicken house. You have been in my home; you have slept on my blanket. I want you to tell how poor I am, how little I have in my house.''

The unerring sagacity of this untutored chieftain in reading the hidden motives of his professed friends is well attested by the

Cloven Hoof

betrayed in the following which until this writing, was known only

gum-shoed through Congress without the knowledge or consent of the Yakimas; as attested in a letter of protest from Chief Weyallup Wayacika to Indian Commissioner Leupp, Nov. 10, 1905, and the Commissioner's reply thereto fourteen days later.

The money expended in "irrigation works" or other improvements on the Yakima Reservation prior to the passage of the Jones bill in question, was from the Annual Indian Appropriation bill, and was non re-imbursable; and to charge the Indians up with it was a gross repudiation. The Yakimas have never understood this "settle-ment" (?) but they realize that the white man has settled within their Reservation and that the Government has played them false. They bitterly resent this injustice and I have heard the topic warmly discussed in the tribal councils. It has ever been a barrier to the success of the Wapato Project.

On October 6, 1909, the Indian Council wired Indian Commissioner Valentine:

"Council Yakimas now in session regarding water rights. They desire to know whether boundary matter in Cedar Valley has been settled; if so, what amount al-lowed Indians therefor." * * *

The Commissioner wired reply:

"* * * Claim of Indians to tract of land in Cedar Valley was recognized by Act of Congress, December twenty-one, nineteen four." * * *

This message did not contain the information most desired. The crime of repudi-ation whereby the lands settled by the whites were "declared to be fully compen-sated for," was studiously kept in the background. The "Indian factor" had been "eliminated" and was not to be considered.

The following "ultimatum" reveals to what pitch of excitement the tribesmen were wrought by this flagrant violation of their vested treaty rights:

"Yakima Reservation, Council of Yakimas, Nov. 2d, 1909.

"To the Honorable Secretary of the Interior, Mr. Ballinger, Washington, D. C.:

"Dear Sir: We, the undersigned, have this day above dated, considered a long-standing question relative to the Cedar Valley country which has been settled up by the whites and for which the United States has not at any time in our recollection treated with our fathers or with us—and which we have time and again asked the United States to restore to us again as an integral part of our Reservation. We do hereby demand an indemnity for all moneys paid the United States in money for land entered by settlers in the Cedar Valley country, and as it seems there is no prospect of the country being vacated by such settlers by the United States.

"We also demand the absolute right to control our own Reservation and as we are aware of the fact that our Reservation is an Indian country, set aside by our fore-fathers by virtue of their own right of choice before they ceded the country around it to the United States as an everlasting inheritance, our Reservation is not to be rated as a Government Reservation.

"We also by unanimous voice set aside all right of the government to set aside a small strip of our own country for grazing commons or pasture. We have an abso-lute right to set aside any area of country for such purposes the tract containing two townships for grazing land as set aside for us is not recognized as we have stock which cannot subsist on same. We, therefore, take this means to inform your office of our position in the matter—and until this matter is settled satisfactorily we can not enter other questions now pending.

"Very respectfully."

(Signed by Charley Wesley, acting head chief; Louis Mann, Secretary of Council, and 14 other prominent Indians.)

See Note 9, this volume, for the original petition of the Yakimas concerning tribal stock range.

The Wenatchee scandal, referred to by Chief Yoom-tee-bee, is too great an intrigue for the scope of this work.

to the Indian Department and the cohorts of the Reclamation Service.

"Toppenish, Washington, May 27, 1909.

"Honorable W. L. Jones,
                    Washington, D. C.

"My Dear Jones:

"I presume that you are busy with the tariff, but there is a matter of serious importance which has arisen here. The Reclamation Service are going to take the surveying crews away from the Reservation in a very short time now, unless something definite can be ascertained from the Indian Department. I understand that about $30,000 has been expended in these surveys and the project is in good shape to go ahead, but the Indian Department has not reported any progress in the matter of securing consent of the Indians.

"As you know, the Yakima Reservation presents an ideal situation for getting water on the land quickly and cheaply. Not a flume or syphon and scarcely a cut or fill on the entire project. Most of the land is reasonably near railroad, and would immediately be used for making homes. * * *

A SUMMER HOUSE OF THE YAKIMAS.
Satus River Canyon, Yakima Indian Reservation, 1906.
(Copyrighted by the Author.)

"Mr. Roblin, who was lease clerk at Fort Simcoe for a number of years, came here about last February, as I remember, and stated that his mission here was to get the consent of the Indians to water their lands and sell sixty acres of each eighty-acre tract. He stated to me that he would be here three months for work on this plan. * * * I suggested to him a plan. It was as follows: Attorney Williamson (See Note 8) represented that the Reclamation Service did not like to have the Indians hold twenty acres out of each allotment as, in their opinion, it would greatly injure the project, that is, white people would not want to buy sixty acres out of each eighty-acre tract, leaving the Indian family in possession of the other twenty acres, and he thought that it would be a very much better plan if the Indians could be segregated on some other section of the Reservation and allow them to sell the full eighty acres of each allotment. His idea was that new

NOTE 8.—Mr. Ralph B. Williamson, local attorney for the Reclamation Service.

allotments might be made to the Indians, either in the mountains, or upper valleys or on the Satus where the Indians could go and raise stock and do their farming together. * * *

"Yours,

"H. M. GILBERT."

The stench of this unearthing is nauseating to the nostrils of common decency. None knew better than the Reclamation people and Mr. Gilbert that the lands in the mountains or upper valleys are unfit for farming purposes; that the bleak, barren Cascades where

SCENE ON THE SATUS RIVER, 1906.
River flows through Canyon in the foreground. (Mary Remy, Photo.)

frost and snow holds revelry seven months in the year, was seriously contemplated as the Last Segregation and Final Grave of the helpless Yakima is appalling. It is well that this hellishly inhuman plot was kept from the ears of the home loving and excitable tribesmen.

Soon after the Simcoe Council, I was called to West Virginia by the fatal illness of my aged father, and I know but little of the immediate subsequent events. The questionable methods pursued by the promoters of the Wapato Canal had engendered much bitter feeling among the Indians. Chief Yoom-tee-bee, the recognized leader of the hostiles, could not understand why the whites were permitted to swarm into the reservation, which was "given to us for all time." Their agency affairs were handled very unsatisfactorily, and

TOM-MAN-CHA-TAH-NEE'. KOHPT.
(Falls of the Fish Trap.)
Satus River Canyon, 1906. (Remy.)

their several petitions for redress of grievances elicited only vague promises, or were wholly ignored. The agency inspections were farcial; conducted secretly from the Indians, who were not permitted the opportunity to recite their wrongs. This blind business excited them. The Yakima were only dogs. Wild rumors were current that the reservation was to be thrown open, their lands sold or taken from them, and the streams confiscated by the Reclamation Service. Cattle thieves operated with impunity, and bootleggers plied their nefarious trade. (See Note 9.)

One morning in 1908, while riding with Chief Yoom-tee-bee in the upper part of the Reservation, he dwelt long upon the wrongs suffered by his people through the greed of the white man. He spoke of their treaty rights of 1855, and said, "Long time ago this government

NOTE 9.—In their petition to Secretary Ballinger, August 24, 1909, the Yakimas pray:

"Eighth—That owing to the fact that we are constant losers from thieving stockmen, we are deterred from engaging in extensive stock-raising, no outside grazing permits shall be granted within the boundaries of the Yakima Reservation settlements, and that a sufficient range in the foothills be reserved for our exclusive use.

"Ninth—We implore protection from boot-leggers and demand the removal of all saloons from the Reservation."

This was the second time within the year that the Yakimas had asked departmental relief from the depredations of cattle thieves. Mr. Ballinger agreed with the Indian Council that he would set aside a pasture range for their exclusive use, and did so; but the boundary proved so inadequate and worthless, that the tribe refused to recognize its validity. (Refer to Note 7, this volume.)

The Secretary regarded the Reservation saloons and boot-leggers of such trifling moment that he wholly ignored this part of the petition. The first is a "necessary" adjunct to the building and development of the Reservation towns, while the last is a "Good Indian" making auxiliary, to be endured.

and Gov. Stevens made treaty and took all our land but this reservation. This, Gov. Stevens said, should be ours as long as the sun shines and the water flows; and no white man would be allowed to live on our reservation." Ascending a slight emience where the vision was unobstructed, he pointed tragically to the east, where in the distance could be seen the fringe of settlements marking the irrigated district, and exclaimed, "You see there the houses of the white man. They are built on the land of my people. The Government has lied; the white man is fast owning our lands. If the Government must have my reservation, I will sell all under the ditch and keep all on this side. No white man must come here. The good Indians will move up here, and we will keep out all saloons. By and by the drunk Indians will all die, and there will be no more trouble."

REV. STWIRE G. WATERS.
Ordained Minister M. E. Church, 1871.
Elected Head Chief of the Yakimas
March 22, 1916.
"I have been praying that the Lord
would send a good man to help us."

The Soda Springs, located a short distance from the agency, because of their medicinal properties have always been a favorite resort of the Indians, especially the aged and infirm. This sylvan retreat had been practically usurped by the whites until no Indian could camp there with any degree of satisfaction.

A Tribal Council.

At a tribal council, July 1, 1910, Chief Waters stated that the Superintendent had on three different occasions insisted that these springs with their forty-acre reserve be sold. The Chief objected. "We cannot," said he, "dispose of this to the whites. We have young people capable of improving these springs." The chief continued, "I found a log house built at these springs and asked Mr. Young to have it destroyed, but he gave me no satisfactory answer."

Louis Shuster, an aged tribesman, said: "This world is the work of Me-yah-wah (God). Of course this God is above us and has great power. He hears us talk and knows if we are speaking the truth or telling lies. We rely on you to send a full report to the Department for us. We feel glad over this. When the whites were few our fathers gave them land. Today I see those few white people grown strong and prosperous. For them I am glad. I feel well towards all, but I grieve to see my people broken and scattered by those whom we befriended. I, a red man, am in poverty and not prosperous. The government gave

"JIM" MENINOCK (Meninokt).
Son of Chief Meninock, signer of
Treaty, 1855.

us breeches and blankets, but they are faded and gone. We do not ask that these be replaced. We want only our own and the right to live."

Judge Simpson then said: "I will tell in a few words what I know. The Agent seems to look upon us as ignorant children. He is telling us that our lands will be bought, and is asking us to sell. We are ignorant and do not know, but he is always telling us this. I corroborate what Chief Waters says concerning the reserve. We do not want to sell any of it. Our older people reserved this for us and we want to reside here. We want to keep it for our children. The government in a treaty with our fathers made witnesses of the sun, the mountains and the rivers that so long as these remain should this Reservation be for them and their children.

"The sun has not grown dim; the mountains have not moved; the rivers still flow; but our Reservation has changed and is slipping from us.

"Another question put up to us is the water. These creeks flowing through our Reservation are ours. They belong to us; also the Yakima River. I claim half of it under our treaty rights. It is ours."

Chief Saluskin, whose primitive training precludes the idea of double dealing, lamented, "My father was once Chief of all this country, and our tribe was strong. * * * * I now see the whites growing rich from our lands while my tribe is going down in pov-

SOCIAL DANCE OF THE YAKIMA.
(Woodfield, 1911.)

erty and dying from whiskey and disease. We want you to help
us. * * * * If we sell our land, we will have no place to go. We
cannot live among the whites."

Distrust rent their own ranks. Among the various leaders of the
fourteen Confederated Tribes which comprise the Yakima, is the
ever haunting fear of treachery. They were, however, practically
united on one score. They would not exchange their allotments for
the water which was theirs by the treaty of 1855. The Jones Bill
was brigandage of the purest type. In the early stages of the
trouble, mutterings and acrid denunciations of the "powers that be"
were heard by one in close sympathy with a certain prominent
chieftain. There loomed above the eastern slopes of the mighty
Cascades, a cloud as dark and ominous as the shadow of death. A

WAR DANCE OF THE YAKIMA, 1911.
(Copyrighted by the Author.)

few desperate spirits conceived the idea of self-sacrifice for what they believed to be the good of the tribe. They would create a status which would so arouse the public as to force an investigation of their tribal condition. Secret councils were held: "medicine" was made, and the whites will never know by what mere chance an actual uprising was avoided. The band fully realized what the war-path meant; that they would be hunted and shot or hanged as out-laws. The motive, right or wrong, was patriotism, born of despair.

In the death of Chief Yoom-tee-bee, March 10, 1910, the Yakimas lost their strongest leader and the Reclamation Service was rid of a determined foe.

The work of securing signatures was continued under somewhat modified tactics; "strays" were occasionally caught, and the list

YAKIMA INDIAN HUNTERS IN CAMP, 1912.
Story Telling while the Venison Broils.
(Copyrighted by the Author.)

of "progressives" added to in various ways. The Indians aver that some of them were induced to sign, believing that it was for the purpose of opening a public road; others, that they were signing for rent money. But despite this despicable double dealing, ultimate success seemed far distant. The Yakimas as a whole were deter-mined. The most sanguine promoters were discouraged. The Wapato Canal was likely to prove only a chimera. Something must be done, and the

Last Desperate Card Was Played.

There are on the Reservation many very capable Indians, who feel that they should be permitted to transact their own private affairs, so far as their individual allotments are concerned, inde-pendent of government supervision. This longing for semi-liberty was now to be taken advantage of in an attempt to further the interests of the Reclamation Service.

In March, 1911, the following letter was sent to two hundred and nine Indians. From a number of these letters in my possession, I

THE INTERVIEW, 1911.
(Copyrighted by Ovid T. McWhorter.)

select the one received by Louis Mann, Corresponding Secretary of the Yakima Indian Council Fire, rancher, house carpenter and harness maker.

"Department of the Interior, United States Indian Service.

"Yakima Agency, Fort Simcoe, Wash., March 9, 1911.

"Mr. Louis Mann,

"North Yakima, Washington.

"Dear Sir:

"Last fall I submitted to the Indian Office for approval, a list containing the names of a number of the most intelligent, industrious and worthy Indians, recommending that they be given the privilege of leasing their own and minor children's allotments. Your name was on this list.

"Recently the list was returned to me advising that no Indian allotte who had not signed a petition for the purchase of a water right under the proposed Wapato Project would be considered competent and be granted authority to lease his or her land. As you have not signed such a petition, I write this to explain to you that I would be glad to resubmit your name to the Office, recommending you as one competent to lease your own land; but in order to do so, it will be necessary that you sign one of the water right petitions in question. If you do not thoroughly understand the nature of these petitions, I would suggest that you call at the Agency whenever convenient, when I will take pleasure in explaining it to you in detail.

"Your early and favorable consideration in this matter will, in my opinion, be to your best interest. A blank is enclosed herewith for your use, if desired.

"Very respectfully,

"S. A. M. YOUNG,

"Supt. & Spec. Disb. Agent."

"P. S.—This only applies to lands within the boundary of said project."

Among those who received this "bid" for the heritage of their intelligence, are Rev. Stwire G. Waters, an ordained minister of the Methodist Church, and Head Chief of the Yakimas; We-Yallup Wa-Ya, Ci-ka, clan chief of the Ahtanum and president of the Yakima Tribal Court; Tecumseh Yakatowit, recently elected head chief by the Anti-brotherhood faction of the tribe. Lancaster Spencer, a man of education and prominence; Mrs. Spencer, two daughters and one son, a private in the United States Army, were also complimented with this offer of a "Mess of Pottage." R. D. Holt, a successful merchant tailor of North Yakima, a graduate of the Chemawia Indian School, Oregon, 1897, holds a teacher's certificate in voice and music theory, Willamette University, Oregon, 1898. Government Instructor in Tailoring, Indian School, Santa Fe, New Mexico; graduate of John J. Mitchell School of Garment Cutting, New York City, 1902. Harry Holt, accountant and bookkeeper. Mrs. Bessie Swartz, holding teacher's certificate, Eighth Grade Public Schools.

CHIEF WE-YAL-LUP WA-YA-CIKA.
"I am not against the white man."
(Copyrighted by the Author.)

Other Yakimas of marked business ability could be added to this list, but suffice to say that this brilliant attempt at coercion failed of its object. In a subsequent council at White Swan, Chief Waters justly demanded of Superintendent Young that he "Send no more such letters to my people." Mr. Young replied that he could not permit Mr. Waters to dictate to him; that the letters in question had been "sent out under instructions from the Indian Department." Louis Mann, the "Bad Injun of the Ahtanum," wrote me concerning this letter. "On great God's earth, I will never under any circumstances do this. If I was born dry, well let me go to hell as I am if I ever under any law sign away my little allotment." "It is a shame," he afterwards said, "that this government would try to bribe and blackmail us in this way. But the white man has no shame. He is blind to all good and like a wolf is hungry for our little homes."

It is hard to conceive that the Indian Department would resort to such questionable means in an attempt to achieve a coveted end. In this it steeped its shrine in the plunder-lust of the land shark and soulless speculator. The smut of crime blackens the act. Is the poor recognition of the Indians' capabilities a thing of barter to be had only at the price of the prerogative to think for himself? After the Yakimas' experience with the promoters of the Wapato Project up to this time, would it be a mark of intelligence had he accepted the proffered "trade"; and by so doing jeopardized his title to three-fourths of his allotment? Let him who is suffering from a preponderance of brains, cast the first stone at the "foolish" Yakima.

LOUIS CHARLES MANN, 1912.
("Bad Injun of the Ahtanum.")
"I am trying to live peaceably and abide by the white man's law."

In the face of the foregoing, it is interesting to note that Louis Mann, of his own volition, leased to Mr. Amos Morse, near White Swan, an inherited eighty acres, 1911 and 1912, for which he received $180.00 cash, per year, in advance. Under date November 11, 1911, Mr. Young served notice on Mr. Morse that

"Since the land has been used by you during the past season without a Government lease, it becomes my duty to collect a reasonable rental for the use of it, and to take it up on the records as trespass money."

The sum asked for is $180.00. Mr. Morse was also notified that he should take a government lease if he wanted the land for 1912, otherwise he would be expected to vacate by March 1, 1912. Later, in response to an inquiry, Mr. Young wrote me:

* * * "The rules and regulations governing the leasing of Indian lands strictly forbid the Indians to lease privately. We have a few competent Indians who are permitted to lease their own allotments without Departmental control. These leases, however, must be approved by me, and one copy furnished the Secretary of the Interior for file. *Louis Mann is not one of the number granted this privilege.* If Mr. Morse uses the allotments of Louis Mann and Lucy Mann during the sea-

son of 1912, without a government lease, this office will compel him, through the
courts, if necessary, to pay trespass into this office." * * *

The Trail of the Serpent

Is still more patent in the following:

"Department of the Interior, Office of Indian Affairs.)
"Washington, May 11, 1912.   }

"Mr. Louis Mann,
"North Yakima, Washington

"My Friend: The office has received your letter of January 29, 1912, saying
that you were one of a number of Yakima Indians recommended as being competent to lease their lands and those of their minor children without Departmental
control, and that you do not understand why you have not been given this privilege. You add that you have leased your land and also that of your deceased wife
for $180.00 cash in advance.

"The Superintendent of the Yakima Agency submitted a list of Indians deemed
competent to manage or lease their allotments without Departmental supervision

THE HOME OF LOUIS MANN, "INCOMPETENT."
Built by himself, 1912.
"Ahk-a-nunk Why-am-mah."   (See the Eagle.)
(A snap shot. Copyrighted by the Author.)

and your name was included therein. He was informed, however, that this privilege would not be given to any one who had not signed a petition for a water
right under the Wapato Project. It appears that you have not signed such an
agreement. Notwithstanding this fact, your name was presented to the Department for consideration in connection with the leasing privilege, and on May 2
your request was denied by the Assistant Secretary.

"The lease in question is illegal and void, and unless your renter enters into a
legal lease he must vacate the land.

"Respectfully,
"C. F. HAUKE.
"Second Assistant Commissioner."

For spurning the bribe of March 9, 1911, Louis Mann "is not

one of the number." When speaking of this to me, this fair-minded tribesman said: "I have advised my people and not for one million dollars will I betray or sell them out."

This coercive policy is in keeping with that wherein an allottee who applies for and receives a patent in fee for his land is compelled to sign for water under the Reclamation Service. A purchaser of deceased Indian lands is also forced to apply for water under the same conditions, without any limit as to the probable cost of such water, nor stipulated time of delivery. Such odious tyranny has served greatly to hold land values below par; the Indian alone being the loser.

The following tabulation shows the number of all classes signed for water prior to June 27, 1911:

Competents 132
Minors on account of incompetent parents.............. 57
Incompetent adults 327
Minors, competent parents 69
Minors, orphans 14
Deceased Indians 67

All except those designated "competents" being signed by the Superintendent.

White owners 160
                                              ————
Total 726

This represents about fifty per cent of the land affected, while

WHE-ACH (Sweat House),
Yakima Indian Reservation, 1911.
(Copyrighted by the Author.)

only seventy-five per cent is required to make the Jones Bill effective. Such, doubtless, was the policy defined when two years previous the boast had been made to me that "Within five years the white man will have such control as to enable him to build the canal regardless of the Indians' consent"; and that "The government will build this canal whether the Indians want it or not."

At a public meeting in Toppenish, April 5, 1911, Superintendent Young stated that the public was laboring under a misapprehension relative to the Wapato project; that the petitions then being presented to the Indians provided for a water right, exclusive of selling any part of the allotments watered. I asked for a copy, as I was to attend a tribal council the next day, and pledged that the Indians would sign such petition. It was not forthcoming. Subsequently I repeated this request by letter, and received a duplicate

A PRIMITIVE DWELLING.
Yo-kosh (Deer horn) and Wife—Yakima Indian Reservation.
(Photographed, Dec., 1911.)

of the old petition, in previous use. Mr. Young in his letter of transmittal says:

"I trust after reading this blank carefully and understanding it, that you will cease from further opposing this project. We feel that your opposition has been very material in hindering the progress of this work, and since it appears to be the result of a misunderstanding I hope that we can now depend upon your assistance."

Astounded, and believing that Mr. Young had by mistake sent an obsolete copy, I renewed my request for the petition mentioned in his speech, pledging to "secure the consent of my tribe for the earliest possible commencement of the work." Result—an exact duplicate of the former copy. Despairing of ever being able to fathom the ways of the white man, I felt that perhaps after all the admonition of Chief Klah-toosh at the Fort Simcoe Council was not far fetched.

In several instances the white purchasers of Indian lands have boldly usurped the water running in irrigating ditches built by Indians more than a quarter of a century ago. In 1910 and 1911 Simon Goudy and others near White Swan suffered in this respect. Mr. Goudy lost his potato crops in consequence and when he reported conditions to Superintendent Young, that worthy refused to interfere. Louis Mann on the Ahtanum was a loser from the same cause. The Indian officials were either unable or unwilling to afford relief. On January 27, 1912, the affected allottees petitioned the Secretary of the Interior for protection, and notwithstanding an ''investigation'' was promised, the past season was a repetition of the two previous years—stolen water with even a wider ruination of crops. The ''Bad Injun'' has declared his intentions for the future. ''I am trying,'' he said, ''to live peaceably and abide by the white man's laws. This ditch was built some forty years ago and by my people and it is ours. My wife and papooses must have food same as those of the white man. If the officials cannot pro-

TYPICAL YAKIMA INDIAN DWELLING, 1912.
Home of Schna'-tupsh (Sna'-tupsi Ka-mia, one of the last surviving
warriors, Yakima War, 1855.
(Copyrighted by the Author.)

tect me in my rights, and my ditch is again killed, there is one Injun going on the war path. I will use my rifle.''

In 1911 the Reclamation Service collected $4,200 storage water rentals at $1.00 per acre in excess of fifty cents per acre for canal maintenance. Early in August, 1912 the canal gates were shut down without any justification. Owing to the unusually heavy rains in the mountains and upper valley, the flow of water was more than normal and the white owners and lessees of Indian lands, claiming that there was no need for storage water, refused to accede to this demand for a "pound of flesh," but on the contrary began preparations to test the legality of the action. To avert this storm and the exposures sure to follow, at the last moment the canal gates were raised and "free" water was sent by the Reclamation Service—and perhaps God—to gladden the hearts of both Indian and white rancher.

The yearly canal maintenace fee must be paid by the middle of July on pain of forfeiture of water, which is just under ordinary conditions. Money due allottees from land rentals are withheld, while in many cases the Indian actually suffers in consequence, especially the aged and infirm. Mr. Apes Goudy, an industrious allottee, in 1912 had $2500.00 due him which was held by the Agency, and was refused $20.00 with which to pay his water rental. He saved his forty acres of growing alfalfa only by borrowing the money from a neighbor.

Notwithstanding the Yakimas have timber valued at more than three million dollars, they are unable to make any use of it in building improvements. The sawmill erected by the government in accordance with treaty stipulations, was burned more than twenty years

TYPICAL YAKIMA INDIAN BARN. 1912.
(Copyrighted by the Author.)

ago, under suspicious circumstances, as the Indians declare. Since that time the Indians have been compelled to purchase lumber from local dealers at an advanced price. The great majority of their dwellings comprise one or two single walled rooms, with a "lean to" kitchen; while their "barns" are cottonwood posts planted in the ground, roughly boarded or wattled with poles; thatched with willow brush and straw. They have vainly importuned the Indian office to have this saw mill repaired. Under date of April 26, 1909, in answer to an appeal from Louis Mann, Mr. Hauke wrote: "The sawmill is to be put into shape for operation at an early date." This promise is now almost three years old and the "early date" is still in the future. No attempt has been made towards restoring the mill.

The Yakimas' complaint of unfair dealing covers practically every phase of the development of their reservation. Bitter feelings attended the adjustment of damages for the right-of-way for the Toppenish, Simcoe and Western Railroad. It is averred that many allottees unwittingly signed settlement papers, supposing that they were "signing for lease money." It would appear from the affidavit of Pauline Pims, March 1, 1911, that this is true. Others charge that coercive and intimidative methods were resorted to in securing signatures. Mr. Simon Goudy, a half-blood, and one of the 209 offered a "competency" tag in exchange for an autographic application for water under the Jones Bill, refused to accept the appraisement of $183.00 damages to his lands as returned by Supt. Young and a representative of the railroad company, and incurred divers troubles therefrom. It would appear from Mr. Goudy's affidavit, Feb. 28, 1911, that he was first asked by Supt. Young to donate the right-of-way in question, and that afterwards when he refused the appraised valuation, Mr. Young sent, on three different occasions, Indian policemen to forcibly bring Mr. Goudy to the Agency for the purpose of compelling him to sign the right-of-way papers. These measures failed and the case was referred to a board of appraisers for adjustment and in due time Mr. Goudy was notified by Mr. Young that the damages had been re-assessed at $381.25. This Mr. Goudy agreed to accept, but when he called at the Agency for the money, he was informed that $20.00 of the amount must go to the appraisers. Mr. Goudy refused settlement and the transaction was not closed until several months later, when, at my instance, it was brought to the notice of the Indian Department so forcibly that the full amount was ordered paid. The coercive measures pursued by Mr. Young in the premises are verified by a verbal statement from the captain of police, which accompanied the said affidavits in charges preferred against Mr. Young, signed by Louis Mann and the writer, March 2, 1911. These charges lay hidden in the office of the Board of Indian Commissioner until February, 1912, when through the efforts of Senator Miles Poindexter the Indian Department was forced to take notice of the petition. (See Note 10.)

NOTE 10.—"Ahtanum Res., Wash., but my postoffice address North Yakima, Wash., Jan. 20th, 1912.

"Miles Poindexter: My kind and welcome friend, I was reading yours to L. V. McWhorter in relative to Toppenish and Simcoe Western Railway Co., and the charges to [against] Supt. S. A. M. Young, making the poor redskins to sign without their understanding what they sign for and it is a shameful deed for any person to do such business. * * * but of course he will be well guarded by his friends at Washington, D. C., at the headquarters in the office, and what can a poor bl Indian do when the reports are made against him.

"I am not mad at Supt. S. A. M. Young; he is my good friend in person; but as the poor Indians make complaint against him about their moneys the proceed derived from the sales of the inherited lands he holds the moneys and the poor Indians call for their moneys, but he refuse to give them only as he damn please, and in my opinion as I study all of these things doings of the law of United States it is a good Political Schemes. I think this is a good Grafting policy but to a poor Indian he sells his inherited holdings and then wants money but is held down and it seems to me it is merely good Speculation to do away with Indian Country but us poor Indians we do not know and my wish to you is for aid. I wish all of these

On this score, Mr. Hauke, the Second Assistant Indian Commissioner, under date February 24, 1912, wrote Mr. Poindexter:

"In regard to the charges of coercion, the Superintendent in a report dated January 19, 1911, says:

" 'In conclusion, I wish to say that no Indian has ever been forced or unduly urged to sign any paper under my jurisdiction, and all Indians connected with right-of-way damages have been fully advised as to their rights. Moreover, these Indians know their rights too well to be forced into signing what they do not wish to sign, even were I inclined to force them.' "

This bare statement by the Superintendent has recognized preponderance over any affidavits or evidence produced by the Indians, and no investigation of the charges preferred against the Superintendent in the premises was made. However, he has been removed to fresh pastures.

During this time Mr. Goudy had trouble with the railroad construction gang. He justly refused admission to his premises until his claim for damages was settled. One evening representatives of the company informed him: "We will come and pull down that fence to-morrow." "I don't think you will; I will be there," was the quiet reply. At the appointed time a foreman of construction appeared with the ostensible purpose of carrying out the threat of the previous evening; but when he found Mr. Goudy, a committee of one, on reception with a Winchester, he hesitated. For a moment he stood viewing the grim, silent Indian, then became suddenly conscious that he was not living up to the "golden rule," as edging away he said in a conciliative voice, "I was sent here to take down your fence, but I am not going to do it. I don't think it would be right."

SIMON GOUDY, 1912.
"I don't think you will; I will be there."
(Copyrighted by the Author.)

The Jones Road Bill.

In pursuance of a petition from the Commercial Club of Wapato, a Reservation town, and other valley towns, Senator W. L. Jones, under date of January 13, 1911, introduced in the United States Senate an amendment to the Current Indian Approbiation Bill:

"For the construction and improvement of wagon roads on the Yakima Indian Reservation, one hundred thousand dollars to be re-imbursable out of the proceeds from sales of surplus lands of said reservation."

In a communication to the writer, April 28, 1911, Mr. Hauke is free to sanction this measure, stating reasons why the office believes that the appropriation will benefit the Indians. His argument betrays a lack of knowledge of conditions on the Reservation. Owing to the common interests of the Indians and whites, and the diversified interests of the many allottees, no adequate justice to the Yakimas as a tribe could come in the passage of this bill and the Indians were greatly incensed. It was "another scheme of the white man to steal our money."

Under date February 27, 1911, the Commercial Club of Toppenish petitioned the Secretary of the Interior, urging the commencement of the Wapato Project, stating that "the Indians have expressed themselves and are ready and anxious for the work to proceed." This petition is voluminous and dwells on the importance of immediate action in order to avoid litigation, citing that the shortage of water for irrigation purposes the previous season had caused a fund to be raised and an attorney employed to bring suit in the name of the Indians for their water rights. "Active pleadings by interested property owners alone averted" this long dreaded litigation, which would have a tendency to depreciate land values throughout the valley. The petition emphasizes that the Indian be permitted to sell some part of his holdings; and repeats the same old gag that the "white home owners would wield a splendid influence over their Indian neighbors."

The road bill in question was presented without consulting the

MRS. JOSEPHINE AUGUSTUS YEM-OWAT, (1912)
The last surviving child of Tee-ias (Tee-ya-yash) Peace Chief of the Yakimas, 1855.
(Copyrighted by the Author.)

Yakimas, nor were they aware of this new move to relieve them of their tribal wealth, until I received a copy of the bill from Washington. A council of the tribe was immediately called, and a hurried counter-petition signed by fifty-three Indians, was forwarded to the Commissioner of Indian Affairs. Superintendent Young had previously committed himself not to oppose this

Swing of the Big Commercial Stick.

He was tied so far as the interests of his wards were concerned.

April 6, 1911, the Yakimas, at my instance, assembled in Council and forwarded a petition to the Indian Office, asking for the construction of the Wapato Canal by the Indian Department, and briefly outlined a plan by which they think the work can be done. Tribal funds are to be used, but no part of any allotment watered is to be taken for any cost of the canal, but if any allottee benefited has not tribal or individual money to cover costs, the products or rental of the allotment so watered is pledged for such cost. They are not to pay for any storage dams. The petition also provides that the $100,000 called for for road building, is to be used in the construction of the canal.

Owing to the strong protest by the Indians and the publicity therefrom, the road bill never reached the floor of the Senate. It remains to be seen what disposition was made of their petition for the Wapato canal.

Under date of June 10, 1911, Mr. Hauke, in reply to this petition, wrote me:

TW-WAH-Y.
Christianized "Flora,"
Six-months-old Yakima, 1911.
(Copyrighted by the Author.)

"The matter of securing funds for continuing the Wapato Project is now before the proper officials for consideration. As soon as all reports in the matter are received, the Office will be in a position to outline a program for the future irrigation of the Yakima Reservation."

In September, 1911, Hon. Walter F. Fisher, Secretary of the Interior, accompanied by Senator W. L. Jones, met the Yakimas in council at Toppenish for the ostensible purpose of hearing their side of the water rights question. I was then absent from the state, but Mr. Fisher was handed a written statement, signed by myself and William Charley, that: "We have proof that deception has been practiced in securing signatures of the Yakimas for water rights under the Wapato Canal."

But, of course, such a charge emanating from "two mere Indians" could not be considered. I am creditably informed that apparently the Secretary was possessed of all desired facts in the case and was ill disposed to hear any complaint from the Indians. The meeting proved one of mere form; the policy of irrigation for the Reservation had been previously determined.

HANNAH.
Three Years Old; Yakima (1911).
(Copyrighted by the Author.)

Suppressing a Just Measure.

On February 22, 1912, Hon. J. H. Stephens, Chairman of the House Committee on Indian Affairs, in the interests of the Yakimas and the Pimas, who are similarly situated, introduced in the House H. J. Resolution No. 250:

"Providing for institution of suits by the Attorney General to determine and adjudicate the rights of the Pima Indians to the use of the waters of the Gila river and its tributaries in Arizona and New Mexico for irrigation purposes, and to determine and adjudicate the rights of the Yakima Indians to the use of water for irrigation of Ahtanum creek and the Yakima river and its tributaries in the State of Washington, and for other purposes."

This resolution was referred to the Committee on Indian Affairs and ordered printed. It was then sent to Secretary Fisher for approval, who held it in abeyance.

The Jones Storage Water Bill.

In the meantime other measures touching the vital interests of the Yakimas were on foot. On May 2, 1912, Senator Jones introduced in the Senate S. Bill No. 6693, appropriating $1,600,000

"For the purpose of constructing storage reservoirs to impound flood waters of the Yakima river to provide one thousand five hundred cubic feet of water per second of time at the Reservation gates for the irrigation of one hundred and twenty thousand acres, more or less, on the Yakima Indian Reservation * * * to be expended in said works by the Reclamation Service."

While this appropriation is not reimbursable from the Yakima tribal fund (which for the fiscal year 1912 was $35.11), the import of the bill is to destroy the riparian rights of the Indian and the appropriation of 1000 cubic feet by Agent Lynch, and to clinch forever the Reclamation's hold on the Reservation. There is, however, a provision wherein "to the extent of thirty-two thousand acres, estimated to be necessary for the support of Indians allotted within the project, for which a water supply of four hundred cubic feet per second of time is required, shall receive water free of any and all cost of said storage works."

This estimate is based upon the computation of four hundred Indian families within the radius of the proposed irrigation system, with four members to the family, or 1,600 all told. This is "free water" for twenty acres for each Indian, and all the other land must remain dry, or pay for water at whatever price the Reclamation Service is pleased to impose. Seemingly, Mr. Jones and the "system" could not get away from the twenty-acre conspiracy of March 6, 1906. How unfortunate that the government was not possessed of this "discriminating talent" in determining the actual "needs" of the Yakimas, when the original allotments were made in 1894.

The bill was passed upon by the Committee on Indian Affairs, and referred to Secretary Fisher for approval. Mr. Fisher in his recommendations on this bill to the committee, June 13, 1912, after reviewing the water situation in the Yakima valley, and the limitation in 1905 of the Reservation waters to 147 cubic feet, says:

"After careful consideration I am of opinion that this limitation was too narrow, and that equitably there should have been reserved to the Indians by authority of the treaty * * * a sufficient flow of water to irrigate an area of land large enough to furnish each Indian family with a farm adequate for its support. Such a farm would be practically worthless in an arid country without sufficient water to irrigate it."

He further states that any attempt to recognize the Indians' claim to the low water flow in excess of 147 cubic feet will result in confusion and litigation; hence the needs of the Indians should be supplied by storage free of cost, "which is the purpose of the pending bill."

Mr. Fisher recommends that the appropriation carry $1,800,000, and that "the bill should provide that the Secretary of the Interior shall designate the particular 32,000 acres that are to receive water without construction charge for storage."

When it is remembered that 32,000 acres within the Wapato canal zone are now under irrigation, of which 24,000 acres belong to allottees, and is, in any event justly entitled to water under the laws of appropriation and usage; this munificent gift of "free storage water" becomes so luminous as to be almost indiscernable.

There is no provision for the distributing system and drainage system contingent to the Wapato Project, but the bill stipulates that these are to be paid for on "such terms as may be fixed by the Secretary of the Interior."

Simultaneous with his report on the Jones bill, Mr. Fisher paid his long delayed respects to Mr. Stephens' Joint Resolution No. 250.

YAKIMA TRIBAL WEDDING SCENE, 1911.
Bridal Party Arriving with Gifts.
(Copyrighted by the Author.)

While admitting that under the treaty of 1855 the Yakima Reservation is riparian to the Yakima river, he attacks this resolution; contending that the limitations and settlements of the Yakimas' right to water for irrigation by the government in 1905 was done authoritatively and

"Upon the faith of this limitation and these agreements large sums of public and private money have been expended in irrigation and irrigation works which would be greatly jeopardized if the said limitation is successfully attacked.

"It is believed," he continues, "that the Secretary, as an incident to his administrative power over the Indians and the public lands reserved for them, may fix the maximum quantity of water necessary for the use of the Indians and which should be equitably reserved for their future use, and may authorize appropriation by others of the unused flow in excess of that maximum. Such limitations of the amount of water reserved for future use by the Indians without present beneficial use have been made in the past and I am of the opinion that the power to make them exists   *   *   *

"I am of the opinion that the institution of any proceedings which would deny the legal basis of the Department's action in limiting the Indian water rights or would deny authority in any Secretary to make reasonable limitations of this character would be contrary to public interests. Upon the contrary, Congress should set at rest all doubt as to such authority in all cases subject to Congressional action by passing an act expressly conferring such authority upon the Secretary."

The Secretary also acknowledges the inadequacy of the water set aside in 1905 for the Yakimas; but argues that the deficiency "should be supplied by storage at public expense," and that "Senator Jones has introduced a bill for that purpose."

Here is an anomaly, grave, yet ludicrous. Mr. Fisher, after twice conceding the injustice of Secretary Hitchcock's ruling, sedately requests that "Congress set at rest all doubt as to such authority." Is

it possible that this Secretary, with his anti-Indian proclivities, deems his mythical "sop" of free storage for thirty-two thousand acres an evidence of infallible justice in the present departmental control of the nation's wards, and that the precedent he thus establishes will govern the actions of his successors? If "gall" is a requisite to office tenure, surely is Secretary Fisher entitled to a life term.

YAH'-YA-TOSH. Ancient Grave.
Yakima Indian Reservation. 1912.
(Copyrighted by the Author.)

From a letter written by Indian Commissioner Robert G. Valentine to the Secretary of the Interior, March 15, 1912, it would appear that the Indian Office has changed base and will contend for enough free water to irrigate all the Yakima Indian lands; and that the distribut-

ing system be constructed under the supervision of the Indian Department, which is compatible with the Yakimas' petition of April 6, 1911.

Pending the Jones bill and the suppression of Stephens' H. J. Resolution, the Yakimas were not wholly idle. Wild Eye, the Fleet Footed, again hit the night trail, but owing to the unfortunate discord among the clans of the tribe, caused by that fake organization,

YAH'-YA-TOSH. Ancient Grave.
Yakima Indian Reservation, 1912.
(Braden.)

"The Brotherhood of North American Indians,"

which was launched by a few mercenary "clam lawyers" during the winter of 1911-12, the Indians could not be united in a general council. The "Brotherhood" following was lured to false security and blinded by the extravagant promises of their "Great Sachem," Richard C. Adams, notorious in the late McMurry Oklahoma Indian contracts scandal, who, they declared, "will look after our interests and is pledged to kill the Jones bill as soon as it is brought up." This promise was a trap. The "Great Sachem" played traitor. It is alleged that he refused to protest against the Jones bill. If it passed, he held contracts from the Yakimas and would "enter suit to recover damages on percentage."

The Jones bill was incorporated in the general Indian Appropriation bill and as Senator Curtis of Kansas, member of committee on Indian Affairs, had declared his intention to oppose new legislation on the Indian Appropriation Bill, to him, in the absence of Tecumseh, Yakatowit, head chief of the anti-brotherhood faction, on June 2, 1912, Louis Mann, as Corresponding Secretary of the Yakima Indian Council, and Clan Chief We-yallup Wayacika, as Chief Judge of the Tribal Court, in the name of their tribe wired a remonstrance against the Jones bill. They also urged "Pass House Resolution 250 and settle dispute forever."

This was followed by a letter, giving a brief summary of their wrongs:

"In the name of our Tribe of Yakima Indians," they said, "we protest against Senate Bill 6693. It is grossly unjust, depriving us of water rights which are ours by all that is equity between man and man. * * *

"In 1906 Secretary Hitchcock divide water in Yakima River and give us 147 cubic feet, and give Sunnyside Canal 650 feet, leaving several miles of our new ditch dry; and not enough to water good the 30,000 acres watered by our ditches.

"We ask if this is right?

"Our riparian rights are older than those of the white man. This Reservation we were permitted to hold when the Government took all our other land. Water is life and belongs to the earth. Our land is poor without water. The Government has set still and let our water be stolen, and now the Reclamation Service cinch us tight if Jones Bill 6693 becomes law. The Reclamation Service talk two ways; it said water under Tieton Project only cost $60.00 or $63.00 acre, but it cost $93.00 acre. * * * White man is better farmer than Indian. Indian only understands horses and cattle. Reclamation (Service) make high cost water; high cost drainage; Indian cannot pay and land be sold from him. This is what white man want. * * *

"On Ahtanum River divide of our Reservation where white man have most land, the Secretary of Interior gives three-fourths of water to white man. Now when red man have most land to water, he gives nearly all water to white man. This was done and we could not help ourselves. We want only what is right. God wants the white man and the red man to live in peace. We try hard to do right and obey the white man's laws. We want you to help us. * * *

"We want you to stop Jones Bill and make law the Resolution 250. Then Atty. General will settle all justly. If this is not done we are bringing suit in U. S. Court to settle our water rights. We want the white man to be honest and treat us right. Our words are done." (See Note H.)

NOTE H.—This protest is set forth in "Memorial of the Yakima Tribe of Indians Protesting Against Senate Bill 6693" in Document No. 1304, House of Representatives, presented by Mr. Stephens of Texas, Jan. 25, 1913.

A copy of this letter was also mailed to Chairman Stephens. Senator Curtis failed to oppose the Jones bill, which was passed by the Senate, and referred back to the House conference. The protest to Mr. Stephens was more effective. The conference struck out this appropriation, and provided legislation authorizing the Secretary of the Interior to present all available information on the subject to the present Congress. As this, however, merely requires Mr. Fisher to "investigate" and "report" upon his own methods, within his own system, the sequel is foreshadowed.

From the first there was little or no hope that the Stephens resolution would become law. Indeed, it is doubtful if such legislation is necessary, as the Attorney General is vested with full power to institute and maintain such suits. His office has declared its eagerness to protect the Indians and "stands ready to act promptly so soon as it shall have received final advices and recommendations from the Interior Department."

It is safe to predict that if such "advice and recommendations" are necessary to action, they will not be forthcoming from the present head of the Interior Department.

As a last forlorn hope, the Yakimas have submitted an appeal to the Attorney General to institute suit for the recovery of their stolen

INDIANS DRYING SALMON.
White Salmon River, Wash., 1912.

water rights; and if this supplication is ignored, some of the tribesmen have declared their intention to bring suit under the Act of Feb. 6, 1901, (Statutes L. 760), which grants an allottee in such case the privilege of appeal to the courts. This will precipitate the long-dreaded litigation, which, it is hoped will culminate in a congressional investigation. Well may the Reclamation venals quail at the prospective exposure of brigandage and loot so long suffered by the dependent Yakimas. That the Indian Department, at the time and subsequent to the theft of the Reservation waters in 1905, realized that an injustice had been done the Yakimas, is attested in the following:

"Department of the Interior,

"Office of Indian Affairs, Washington, September 28, 1906.

"Louis Mann,

"North Yakima, Washington.

"(through the Superintendent of the Yakima Agency.)

"My Friend:

"In a letter dated August 18, 1906, you presented the troubles the Yakima Indians are experiencing relative to the use of water for irrigation purposes, and you want to know what rights such Indians have.

"In answer, I am wholly unable to tell you what will be the ultimate result of the trouble over this question. It is believed that the Indians have a right to sufficient water to irrigate their allotted lands, but there is not enough water for the needs of all who are dependent on the streams from which the Indians must take their supply. As you are aware there is an effort on foot to harmonize these conflicting claims, and it is earnestly hoped that something will be done in the near future by which the Indians will get a recognized right to a sufficient amount of water for their needs.

"Very respectfully,

"C. F. LARRABEE,

"Acting Commissioner.'

At the Thirtieth Annual Conference of Friends of Indians and Other Dependent Peoples, held at Lake Mohonk, N. Y., Oct. 25, 1912:

Mr. S. M. Brosius, Agent for the Indian Rights Association, read an able paper reviewing the Yakima water rights situation, giving citations wherein the courts had, in similar cases ruled favorably for the Indians. The want of space alone prevents me from giving this paper in full. However, it will be found in the Annual Report, 1912, of the society above mentioned.

After Mr. Brosius' address, the conference approved as a part of its declaration of principles the following paragraph:

"In providing water for irrigation for the lands of the Yakima and other Indian tribes the Government is in duty bound to protect their vested and treaty rights to as full an extent as would be done in cases between citizens. We recommend that, whenever practicable, proceedings should be instituted by the Government to procure a judicial determination of the Indian rights."

Since going to press, Mr. Jones, under date of January 21, 1913, introduced in the U. S. Senate as an amendment to the current Indian Appropriation Bill, H. R. 26874, providing $1,800,000 for the construction by the Reclamation Service of storage water reservoirs for the Wapato Project, on practically the same conditions as his former Bill 6693; except that in the new bill eighty per centum of the allotted, and a like per centum of deeded lands within the Wapato unit must be pledged for the cost of the work, and all other claims to a water right must be waived before any part of the work will be commenced.

There is, however, in addition to the twenty-acre free water right to each allottee, a "sop" held out to the owners of lands to which the Indian title has been extinguished, wherein the Secretary of the Interior shall "equitably adjust" their claims to a water right.

Secretary Fisher, true to our prediction, stands firmly by his former position and strongly recommends the passage of the pending bill, which has been recommended by the Senate committee on Indian Affairs.   Both allottees and white owners—the latter through the Reservation Water Users Association—of lands within the Wapato unit have protested against the bill in question, and have asked that the Department of Justice settle through the courts the Reservation's contention for prior rights to the waters of the Yakima river.

This is the first time in the history of the Reservation that the white residents have ever raised their voice against any legislation that looks to the despoiling of the Indians. At the last moment, and when almost too late, they realize that their threatened water right interests, at least, are mutual, and that they have been deceived as to the actual intents of the United States Reclamation Service.

THE CHALLENGE.
WAH-NOK-PI, THE YAKIMA—"A Dream of the Past."

"Lurks in Ambush Along the Trail."

In November, 1911, there suddenly appeared on the Yakima Indian Reservation the Hon. Harve H. Phipps, attorney of Spokane, Washington, who ostensibly promulgated the banding of all the nation's wards into one great faction, "The Brotherhood of North American Indians." He unfolded a plan by which "good, honest" attorneys, regularly employed on percentage, would protect, in the halls of Congress and the courts of justice, not only the jeopardized water rights of the Yakimas, but all treaty guarantees wherein the government has proven recreant to its trust. The time for such a movement was most opportune. The very atmosphere of the Reservation was redolent with trouble and many of the Yakimas were quite ready to listen to the extravagant promises held out by the glib stranger. So cunning were his words that one faction went wild over the prospect of restored Indian rights. They eagerly signed the iron clad "power of attorney and fee agreement" produced by the wily lawyer, wherein he and Richard C. Adams of Washington, D. C., conspicuous in the $3,000,000 Oklahoma McMurry Indian contracts swindle, are to conduct all legal transactions, individual and tribal, on a percentage basis.

Chiefs Stwire G. Waters, Saluskin We-owikt, Lesh-hi-hit and Alex Teio, with Thomas Yallup and Nealy N. Olney as interpreters, were chosen as delegates to Washington where the Brotherhood would be completely organized.

At the Capitol, under the guidance of the Hon. Phipps, the Yakimas, with delegates from other tribes, met Mr. Adams, who blinded them with absurd visions of retrieved tribal power and political prestige. He held out to them the lure of controlling the ballot in seventeen states and dictating the election of 34 senators and 70 representatives. To accomplish this "the tribes must stand as one," and to this end Mr. Adams organized his "Brotherhood of North American Indians," with himself as

"Great Sachem."

This momentous event was heralded to the western tribes in a pompous telegram signed by the Hon. Phipps, "attorney for the Indians," stating in part:

"Brotherhood of North American Indians completely organized. The convention, by unanimous vote, elected Richard Adams of this city as Great Sachem, Joseph Craig of Oregon as Great Secretary. Brotherhood memorials presented to President and to Congress this morning. Indian Commissioner approves of movement."

The constitution of the Brotherhood is liberal. Squaw men, senators, congressmen, judges and any political boss with the prefix "Hon." may join as honorary members.

The Yakima delegates returned home elated. They gave glowing accounts of the power and wisdom of the Great Sachem—the Moses of the Tribes, the Solomon of Councils. By the mere lifting of his weasel-skin bedecked grandfather's cane, the insignia of his office, Carnegie had been induced to pledge $750,000 for the purpose of erecting near the White House a palatial Council Lodge for the Brotherhood. The Great Sachem would reside there and keep watch over Congress and the Indian Department. There would be no more Jones bills to despoil them of lands, water and tribal money. The Yakimas could now work their ranches, roam the mountains, hunt and fish with no concern for the future. They had empowered the Mighty Sachem to care for their interests. He would compel the government to recognize and redress their many wrongs. Ancient tribal glory would be revived and the Reservation maintained for the Indians only. Free water for irrigation purposes, the immediate distribution of vast sums of tribal moneys, unmolested hunting on the public domain, the protection of their fast disappearing berry patches and root areas and the restoration of the Columbia river salmon fisheries were the part to be achieved by the Great Sachem and the Brotherhood.

The Indian Millenium Was Dawning.

With such lure, about 500 Yakimas, many of them children, joined the Brotherhood, while perhaps 100 signed the power of attorney contracts. At the solicitation of the Great Sachem, Chief Saluskin We-ouikt, with Interpreter Yallup, made a second trip to Washington, and after the annual "Feast of the New Food," the following spring, the Chief, with Alex

Teio and Harvey Schuster, again returned. In all eleven passages to the Capital and return were made by these delegates, the entire cost amounting to about $3,300, being defrayed by subscription among the Brotherhood following, many of whom were in penury. To raise this money, guns, horses, saddles and other property was pawned, never to be redeemed. No good came of these expensive junketings. On the other score, the delegates came home with minds confused and warped by the romantic promises made by the forked-tongued Sachem. It was schemed by Adams to ensnare all the tribe, but unfortunately for his purpose, there were a few who refused to be "sweetened" by his words. They saw the stupendous graft concealed in the signed contracts; and the Brotherhood was only a "blanket blind" to beguile them to certain financial ruin. It was suspected that the move was fostered in the interests of the "system." To this body, the Yakima had become too obstreperous; his cry must be hushed. The word "Brotherhood" was insidious, magical. Like the wing of the vampire vibrating, it would cool the wound and soothe the victim while his life blood was being slowly but surely drained. So baleful was the influence of the Great Sachem, that in midwinter, Mr. S. A. M. Young, the Superintendent of the Agency, advised the Indians against his machinations. The Anti-Brotherhood faction was early aroused to the danger and on January 27, 1912, sent the following protest to the Indian Commissioner, signed by Chief Weyallup Wayacika and fifty other Indians, Louis Mann, Secretary of Council:

PETITION.

Yakima Indian (Res.), Wash. }
White Swan, Jan. 23, 1912. }

The Honorable, Commissioner of Indian Affairs.

Washington, D. C.

Sir: We, the undersigned, members of the Yakima Tribes of Indians, hereby protest against the power of attorney and contract and assignments which Harve H. Phipps, of Spokane, Wash., and Richard C. Adams, of Washington, D. C., have been inducing members of our tribes to sign since we believe the activity of these parties has been solely for the amount of money they can get out of it. Furthermore we wish to state that we do not have confidence in the brotherhood which these men are trying to organize among ourselves and other Indians, believing that such organization is for a selfish purpose. We further request that the Indian Office send out word to other tribes of Indians in the United States warning them of these people."

On March 18, 1912, this faction elected as "Head Chief of all the Confederated Tribes of the Yakimas," Tecumseh Yakatowit. This "revolution by ballot" was silently ignored by Chief Waters and his following. The tribe was hopelessly divided—a point gained for the "system."

So-Called Carnegie Donation a Fraud.

But a day of reckoning was coming. The charge of the Great Sachem's treachery in not opposing the passage of the Jones Bill No. 6693 was disclosed to his followers. The alarm spread over the Reservation, and membership to the Brotherhood at one dollar a head ceased. The unused "power of attorney" blanks left by the Hon.

Phipps to be filled in and signed, were destroyed. Frank Meacham, a Carlisle Yakima, hurried to the Warm Springs and successfully warned that tribe. Rumors from the East repudiated the Carnegie donation, and it devolved upon Louis Mann and Chief Weyallup Wayacika, the Watch Dogs of their Tribe, to confirm this report. They wrote Mr. Carnegie as follows:

"Yakima Indian General Council,
"Yakima Indian Reservation, Washington, June 1, 1912.

"Mr. Andrew Carnegie,
"New York.

"Our Friend:

"We are in the dark and ask you to show us light. When our delegates were in Washington, D. C., last winter they were told you subscribed $750,000 to build Council Lodge for Brotherhood of North American Indians. Now report from east to our adopted brother and Tribal Historian, L. V. McWhorter, that you never agree to give this money. We do not like crooked talk and we write you first that we may learn truth. We trust you will let us hear from you soon.

His
X   "WE-YALLUP   WA-YA-CI-KA,
Mark.
"Clan Chief Abtanum Yakimas
"Chief Judge of Yakima Tribal Court."

"LOUIS MANN,
"Corresponding Secretary Indian Council."

"Skibo Castle, Southland, June 25, 1912.

"Mr. Louis Mann,
"Corresponding Secretary Yakima Indian Council.

"Dear Sir:

"Yours of June 1st received. There is no truth whatever in the report that Mr. Carnegie has provided $750,000, or any other sum, with which to build a council lodge for the Brotherhood of North American Indians.

"Very truly yours,

"JAMES BERTRAM,
"Private Secretary."

The power of the Great Sachem's "Tamanawash" was waning. His fake Brotherhood was tottering and to bolster the crumbling fabric, he seized upon the golden opportunity afforded in the recent ruling of the Indian Department, ordering a more liberal disbursement of the allottees' individual moneys, and heralded among the Yakimas and other Western tribes, the following

Bombastic Proclamation.

"Washington, D. C., September 14th, 1912.

"To the members of the Brotherhood of North American Indians and to all other Indians whom it may concern:

"After much work and many persistent efforts the Brotherhood of North American Indians has succeeded in getting an order issued by the Department of the Interior, granting all Indians a more liberal use of their individual moneys deposited in various banks throughout the country and belonging to individual Indians from rentals on their lands, sales of inherited lands and timber, and from other sources.

"While the present order, a copy of which is enclosed, is not as liberal as was expected, or is desired by the Indians, it is far better, and will give the Indians the use of more of their own money than ever before and is a step towards the progress that the Brotherhood was founded to accomplish. We have been beset by many difficulties while securing this order; the President and many of his friends and Senators and Representatives in Congress endorsed the more liberal use by Indians of their moneys and we have received hundreds of telegrams and letters from the Indians urging prompt action. Great credit is due the administration of President Taft for this liberal order and it is certain that the order would not have been issued for several months if the administration had not been thoroughly convinced of our sincerely and earnest purpose in making our demands, and the equity and justice of our cause. In addition, we have been promised that if the Indians make good use of the moneys paid out under the order more liberal treatment will be given in the near future and all Indians will eventually be allowed to have entire control of their individual funds.

"It is hoped that a large delegation will be here on the 6th of December, 1912, from all reservations and Indian settlements in the United States; at that time we hope to pass resolutions and take actions that will result not only in obtaining what we are entitled to in the matter of our individual moneys, but that will result in obtaining for our people, the Indians of North America, more liberty, justice and personal rights now accorded to all other persons, but withheld from the foundation of the Government from the Indian people.

"We feel sure that by close co-operation and help that can be extended by one tribe to another will result in greater progress, advancement, uplifting and the final and complete liberation of our people.

"As Great Sachem of the Brotherhood of North American Indians, I want as many letters as I can get from all Indians, whether members of the Brotherhood or not, expressing the views of our people relative to the best course to pursue for our elevation, advancement and success; and I want these letters addressed to me authorizing me to speak to the President and to other persons in authority, so that, if necessary, they can be used in a memorial to the President and Congress for the benefit of all Indian people.

"Fraternally yours,
"RICHARD C. ADAMS, Great Sachem."

The claim of the self-created Sachem to the honor of instigating and bringing about a long-delayed reform in the disbursement of Indian moneys, in a measure restored the confidence of his wavering followers. Heeding the "Call of the Allies," Chief Waters and Teio, traveling on donated funds, again struck the Trail of the Rising Sun, and sat in the Councils of the Fakir during the Moon of Snows.

As a substance of fact the records of the Lake Mohonk Conference, 1906, shows that Mr. S. M. Brosius there inaugurated and championed the cause in question; since which time the Indian Rights Association and other friends of the Indians have constantly pressed the claim.

Apropos to this is the following communication:

"Department of the Interior, Office of Indian Affairs.
"Washington, November 21, 1912.

"Mr. L. V. McWhorter,
"North Yakima, Wash.

"Dear Sir—
"Your letter of the 11th instant is received, and replying thereto desire to state that from my personal knowledge Mr. S. M. Brosius has for some time past favored a more liberal policy in the disbursement of Indian moneys, both tribal and individual, and advocated such in his address before the Mohonk Conference six years ago.

"I enclose herewith as requested copies of Indian Office circular letters of Sep-

tember 11, 1912, and October 12, 1912, respectively, modifying previous require-
ments in the disbursement of 'individual Indian moneys.'

"Very respectfully,

JAMES McLAUGHLIN,

"Inspector."

Again is the Great Sachem branded an imposter and for the second
time have the Yakimas followed in the wake of this false prophet. It
is certainly incumbent upon the Indian Department to honor the request of the Anti-Brotherhood Council, investigate and warn all the
tribes against the schemes of this consummate grafter, who, like the
deadly Wahk'-puch, lurks in ambush along the trail and strikes with
poisoned fang the unwary.